Where Do Plants and Animals Live?

HOUGHTON MIFFLIN HARCOURT

PHOTOGRAPHY CREDITS: (c) ©Thomas Kitchin & Victoria Hurst/Canopy/ Corbis; 3 (b) ©kaphotokevm1/Fotolia; 4 (c) ©Getty Images Royalty Free; 6 (l) Greg Dale/National Geographic/Getty Images; 6 (r) ©Radius/SuperStock; 7 (l) ©Radius Images/Alamy Images; 7 (r) Getty Images/Photodisc; 9 (t) ©Thomas Kitchin & Victoria Hurst/Canopy/Corbis; 10 (l) ©Getty Images; 10 (r) ©Steve Klics/Fancy/Corbis; 11 (l) ©Photodisc/Getty Images; 11 (c) © BYphoto / Alamy; 11 (r) ©Corbis

Printed in Mexico

ISBN: 978-0-544-07225-1

12 13 14 0908 21 20 19 18 17

4500660628   A B C D E F G

Be an Active Reader!

 Look at these words.

living things	reproduce
nonliving things	shelter
environment	food chain

 Look for answers to these questions.

What are living things?

What are nonliving things?

What is an environment?

Where do plants and animals live?

How do plants and animals get food?

What is a food chain?

What are living things?

Plants, animals, and people are living things. Plants and animals need food, water, and air. Plants and animals also grow and change. Living things reproduce. They make young that look like themselves.

These lion cubs need space to move and grow.

What are nonliving things?

Nonliving things are things that do not need food and water to live. They do not need air and space to live. Nonliving things do not reproduce or make new living things like themselves.

Rocks do not have needs.

What is an environment?

An environment is all the living and nonliving things in a place. This container is called a terrarium. It is an environment for a pet turtle.

The terrarium has living and nonliving things. The turtle and plants are living things. The rocks and water are nonliving.

This turtle can meet its needs in this environment.

Where do plants and animals live?

Plants live in different environments. A forest is one place where plants grow. A forest can have many trees and other plants. A desert is another place where plants grow. Deserts get very little rain. Some deserts are hot.

A forest can have tall trees and small plants.

A cactus is a desert plant.

Some fish use other animals as shelter.

A bird builds a nest on a tree branch.

Animals live in different environments, too. Animals can live on land or in water. Some animals live in both places!

Many animals use plants for a shelter. A shelter is a place where an animal can be safe. Some birds use a tree as a shelter. They eat nuts from the trees. Fish live in water. They need shelter, too.

How do plants and animals get food?

All living things need food to live and grow. A plant makes its own food. It uses light from the sun to make food.

The roots of a plant hold it in the ground. The roots take in water and nutrients. Nutrients help the plant to grow.

A plant's parts help it to live and grow.

flower

stem

leaf

roots

Black bears eat plants and animals.

Animals are different from plants. They get food in other ways. Many animals eat plants. A giraffe eats a tree's leaves and twigs. Many animals eat meat from other animals. A tiger eats meat. Some animals eat plants and other animals!

What is a food chain?

Plants and animals need one another to live. A food chain shows how energy moves from plants to animals.

A food chain begins with the sun. Plants use light from the sun to make food. The food is broken down to give plants the energy they need to grow.

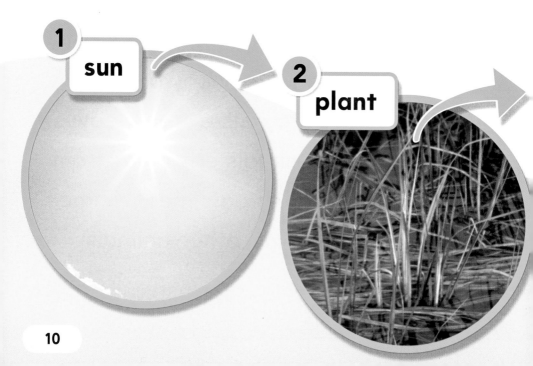

1 sun

2 plant

An insect eats a plant. The insect lives near the surface of the pond. Next a small animal eats the insect. Larger animals live near the pond. They need living things in the pond. A larger animal eats the smaller animal.

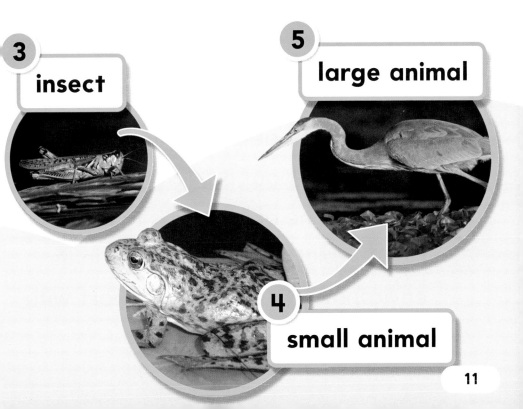

3 insect

5 large animal

4 small animal

Sort the Pictures

Cut out magazine pictures of living and nonliving things. Glue each picture onto an index card. Write a label for each picture. Sort the cards into two piles: living things and nonliving things.

Write a Report

Read a book about an animal you like. Write about its environment. Tell what the animal likes to eat. Draw a picture of the animal in its environment. Share your report with a friend.